6.5

1 point

W9-BSK-113

Colin Powell

Mary Englar

Chicago, Illinois

For information, address the publisher:
Raintree, 100 N. LaSalle, Suite 1200, Chicago, IL 60602

Printed and bound in China by South China Printing Company.
10 09 08 07 06
10 9 8 7 6 5 4 3 2 1

Library of Congress Cataloging-in-Publication Data

Englar, Mary.
  Colin Powell / Mary Englar.-- 1st ed.
      p. cm. -- (African-American biographies)
  Includes bibliographical references and index.
  ISBN 1-4109-1038-5 (hc) 1-4109-1122-5 (pb)
  1. Powell, Colin L.--Juvenile literature. 2. Statesmen--United
States--Biography--Juvenile literature. 3. African American
generals--Biography--Juvenile literature. 4. Generals--United
States--Biography--Juvenile literature. 5. United States.
Army--Biography--Juvenile literature. I. Title. II. Series: African
American biographies (Chicago, Ill.)
  E840.5.P68E54 2005
  327.73'0092--dc22

                              2005004858

Acknowledgments
The publisher would like to thank the following for permission to reproduce photographs:
p.4 Corbis/Reuters/Mohamed Hammi; p.6 Corbis/Lorenzo Ciniglio; pp.8,11,13,15,16,19,21,23,24,27,30,48 Corbis/Sygma; p.28 Corbis/Joseph Schwartz; pp.32, 37 Corbis/Bettman; p.35 Rex Features; p.38,44 Corbis; p.40 Corbis/Peter Turnley; p.42 Corbis/Wally McNamee; p.47 Corbis/Sygma/T.Orban; p.50 Corbis/David Butow; pp.52,54, 56 Corbis/Reuters.

Cover photograph: Rex Features/Greg Mathieson

Some words are shown in bold, **like this.** You can find out what they mean by looking in the Glossary.

Contents

Colin Powell served as President George W. Bush's secretary of state. This is the highest government position achieved by any African American in United States history.

Introduction

Colin Powell is an American success story. From his childhood in a tough Bronx neighborhood in New York City, Powell rose to the highest position in the United States military. He has worked for four U.S. presidents. In his position as the U.S. secretary of state, he faced the most frightening enemies the United States has ever known.

Powell decided on a career in the U.S. Army while he was in college. Before the law was changed in 1948, the U.S. military kept African-American and white soldiers separate. African-American officers were not allowed to be in charge of white soldiers. They were also not allowed to live in the same buildings. They ate in separate dining halls.

By the time Powell joined the Army in 1958, African-American soldiers had the same rights as white soldiers. Powell has said that he believes he was always treated fairly by the military. Even though in 1958 some restaurants in the South refused to serve him because he was African-American, in the military he was **promoted** to higher positions based on his knowledge and skills. Powell admired the Army and was grateful to the opportunities it gave him.

Today, Colin Powell is a role model for all Americans. His success encourages young people of all races to work hard, be honest, and never stop trying to achieve their dreams.

As secretary of state, Colin Powell is pictured listening to speeches at a meeting of the United Nations on February 14, 2003.

In His Own Words

"There is no country on Earth that is not touched by America . . . and there is no country in the world that does not touch us."

"Learn how to get along with different kinds of kids. Make sure you respect other people's religion, race, color, and creed. . . . When you respect somebody else and value their opinion, then you're able to solve problems."

"In one generation, we have moved from denying a black man service at a lunch counter to elevating one to the highest military office in the nation and to being a serious contender for the presidency ... This is a magnificent country, and I am proud to be one of its sons."

". . . I salute the countless thousands of ordinary African Americans who day in and day out, go to work, support their families, and are, along with Americans of all races, the backbone of this country."

"All work is honorable. Always do your best, because someone is watching."

"My responsibility, our responsibility as lucky Americans, is to try to give back to this country as much as it has given to us."

Colin is shown here as a young boy hanging on the family car.

Chapter 1:
Growing Up in New York City

Colin Powell was born in Harlem, a New York City neighborhood, on April 5, 1937. When he was six years old, his family moved to an apartment on Kelly Street in the South Bronx area of New York City.

Kelly Street was like a small town. Colin never felt different because he was African-American. Most people in his neighborhood belonged to different **ethnic groups.** His neighbors came from Eastern Europe, China, the Caribbean islands, and Italy.

Life at home

Colin's father, Luther Powell, had moved from Jamaica to the United States in 1920. At first, he worked as a gardener in Connecticut. Later, he found a job in New York City working in the stockroom of a women's clothing store. His father worked very hard, was **promoted** to salesman, and eventually ran the entire shipping department.

Colin's mother, Maude Ariel McCoy (her family called her "Arie"), came to the United States from Jamaica in 1924. She lived with her mother who rented rooms in their home. When Luther Powell rented a room from Arie's mother, he and Arie became very close. They married in 1929.

As a child, Colin often watched from his apartment window for his father to come home from work. Luther was always nicely dressed in a suit and hat. He whistled cheerfully as he walked home. He often stopped to say hello to people he saw.

Caribbean migration

Before and during World War I, the United States became a powerful economic force in Jamaica and other Caribbean countries. From 1900 to 1920 there was a large migration, or movement, of workers from Caribbean countries to the United States. At this time, there was also a reduction of European **immigrants**, making the formation of large Caribbean communities more noticeable. Most of these communities formed in places like New York, were there was work for the immigrants. The numbers of Jamaican and other Caribbean immigrants declined between 1920 and 1945.

Colin is shown here with his father, Luther Powell. Colin has said in interviews that many people in the neighborhood he grew up in often came to his father for advice.

Colin's mother worked all day as a seamstress. When she got home, she put on her apron and began to cook and clean for her family. She was always busy. Colin remembers her beautiful, warm smile.

Colin was born in the middle of the Great Depression. This was a time in United States history when many banks and businesses closed. Even before the Depression, it was hard for African Americans to find jobs. Many white people were also looking for work during the Depression. As a result, it was even harder for African Americans to find jobs. Employers wanted to give jobs to white people rather than African Americans. Colin's parents worked hard because they knew they were fortunate to have jobs when other people in their neighborhood faced racial **discrimination**.

Going to school

Colin's parents expected him and his older sister, Marilyn, to get a good education and go to college. Colin wanted to do well in school, but he preferred to play games with his friends, go to the movies, or fly kites. He barely passed third grade. His teacher placed him in a class for slow learners. Colin had the ability to do well, but he simply did not care that much about school.

One of the things Colin liked to do with his friends was imagine he was a soldier fighting in World War II (1939–1945). The United States was at war against Germany and Japan.

Colin and his older sister, Marilyn, are pictured here in front of their Bronx apartment building in 1942. Colin is five, and Marilyn is ten.

Germany was trying to conquer Europe, and Japan, Germany's **ally**, sought to control Asia. It seemed that these countries, along with their ally Italy, were trying to take over the world. Inspired by the stories they heard about battles and war heroes, Colin and his friends built model airplanes, battled with toy soldiers, and pretended to watch for enemy airplanes.

As a boy, Colin learned to try to get along with everyone. He did not know that this would turn out to be important for his later life and career.

In 1950 Colin enrolled at Morris High School with his neighborhood friends. Four years later he graduated with average grades. His parents expected him to go to college, so Colin applied to the City College of New York and New York University. Both schools accepted him. He chose the City College of New York because it cost less money to attend. He decided to major in **geology**, the study of rocks and soil, thinking he could get a good job in oil exploration after graduation.

Colin is pictured here around the time of his high school graduation. Later in life, Powell would seek government funding to expand junior Reserve Officers Training Corps (ROTC) programs in high schools.

Powell is shown here in his ROTC uniform. In was during his ROTC classes that he decided that he wanted to pursue a military career.

Chapter 2:
Finding a Career

During Colin Powell's first year at college, he noticed some students wearing military uniforms. They were members of the Reserve Officers Training Corps (ROTC). Powell decided to join the ROTC because he wanted to make new friends. Plus, the ROTC would help pay for college if he agreed to serve in the United States Army for three years after graduation.

Pershing Rifles drill team

In his ROTC classes Powell studied military history, battle planning, and how to take a rifle apart. He earned As in his ROTC courses and soon joined a **drill team** called the Pershing Rifles. Every Saturday morning the drill team practiced marching, rifle salutes, and rifle spins. They worked hard, and Powell became good friends with many of his teammates. Powell began to think the Army might make a good career for him after all.

When Powell was a junior, he led a **drill team** of eighteen men in a drill competition between teams at other New York colleges. His team won a drill contest with 492 out of 500 points. Powell was a good leader. He was able to bring out the best in his team.

ROTC summer training

In the summer of 1957, Powell went to Fort Bragg, North Carolina, for summer military training. This was the first time Powell had ever been to the South. The South had a history **discriminating** against African Americans. Powell's father warned his son to be careful.

For six weeks, Powell learned to shoot rifles and small cannons. He practiced setting up roadblocks and learning how to hide a camp from an enemy. He also ran and exercised to get into good physical shape. At the end of their training, the new **cadets** were judged on their rifle scores, leadership skills, course grades, and physical fitness. Powell was named best cadet in his company. He came in second for best cadet in the entire camp.

After training was finished, Powell rode home with two cadets from New York City. When they stopped to buy gas along the way, Powell had to use a separate rest room labeled "colored." Some service stations did not have a rest room for African Americans at all.

Powell is pictured here at Fort Bragg, North Carolina. Fort Bragg is located about 75 miles south of Raleigh, North Carolina.

Graduation and basic training

In the spring of 1958, Powell became a second lieutenant in the United States Army. His graduation from college the next day was less important to him. He had decided that if he did well during his next three years in the Army, he would make the Army his career.

After graduation, Powell went to Fort Benning, Georgia, for basic training. On the **base**, he did not feel different because he was an African American. But when he left Fort Benning to go into town, he experienced the same kind of **discrimination** he had experienced in North Carolina. He could shop in the stores, but he could not use the stores' restrooms. And he could not sit down and eat lunch in a restaurant.

Germany: Powell's first assignment

At the end of his military training, Powell was given his first **assignment**. At age 21, he was sent to an American army base in Germany where he was the officer in charge of Combat **Command** B, a group of about 40 soldiers. In the 1950s and 1960s, the United States had many troops in Germany. Their job was to protect Europe from the **communist** government in the Soviet Union.

Back to the United States

In 1961 Powell reported to Fort Devens in Massachusetts as an assistant to Major Richard Ellison. Powell worked well with Ellison. Powell was assigned to a job where he handled mail, officer

Alma Johnson is shown in this picture about the time she and Colin Powell began dating.

promotions, and generally helped the soldiers with any problems. But Powell hated paperwork. He wanted to be in charge of troops.

In November, a friend introduced him to Alma Johnson. Johnson had grown up in Birmingham, Alabama. She had graduated from Fisk University in Nashville, Tennessee, when she was only nineteen years old. She had a good job in Boston working with deaf people.

Powell and Alma liked each other right away. They saw each other almost every weekend. He took her home to meet his family in New York City. Then, in the summer of 1962, Powell heard that he had been chosen as an **adviser** to the South Vietnamese Army. Powell knew very little about Vietnam, but he was excited to serve in a war zone. His **assignment** was to last one year.

Alma and Powell's family were not excited about his new assignment. They worried that he might be killed. Powell asked Alma to marry him before he left. She agreed, and they married in August 1962.

After four months of military adviser training in North Carolina, Powell got on airplane headed for Vietnam on December 23, 1962. Alma was pregnant with their first child.

Alma Johnson and Colin Powell were married on August 24, 1962, at the Johnson family home in Birmingham, Alabama. Four months later, Powell left for Vietnam.

Powell is shown here at the U.S. Army camp in A Shau, Vietnam. The A Shau Valley would become the site of several major battles during the Vietnam War.

Chapter 3:
The War in Vietnam

During his military **adviser** training, Colin Powell was **promoted** to captain. When Captain Powell arrived in Vietnam in 1962, there were 11,000 American military advisers working with the South Vietnamese army. They were helping the South Vietnamese army fight against **communist** troops from North Vietnam.

Fighting in the jungle

Powell was **assigned** to A Shau, a camp near Vietnam's border with the country of Laos. He flew to the camp in a helicopter loaded with soldiers and rice and live chickens for the men at A Shau. From the windows of the helicopter, all Powell could see below him was a thick jungle.

The jungle was a miserable place for the soldiers. Insects buzzed around their heads all day as they walked along the jungle trails. They hiked up mountains and down into river valleys. They were always wet from the heat and from wading across rivers.

Powell and his troops also faced many dangers. Enemy soldiers set traps for them and shot at them from the protection of the jungle. It was as if the enemy were invisible. Powell would hear the shots and look up to find one of his men had been killed.

Stepping in a trap

In late July 1963, Powell and his men were walking along a creek in the jungle. Suddenly, Powell's right foot dropped into a hole and he felt a sharp pain. As he pulled his foot out of the hole, he saw that a sharp bamboo stick had gone through his boot and his foot. Powell knew that the enemy soldiers poisoned the sticks in the traps they set. In much pain, he limped to the medical tent.

By the time he reached the tent, Powell's foot was so swollen, the medical officer had to cut his boot off. His foot had turned purple from the poison. Powell was flown to a local hospital were his foot healed quickly, but he did not go back to A Shau. Instead, he was given a desk job at Army headquarters in Vietnam.

In November, Powell was sent home from Vietnam. Alma met him at the airport in Birmingham, and Powell got his first look at his son, Michael, who was now eight months old.

Back to Fort Benning, Georgia

In 1964, Powell was **assigned** to take the **Infantry** Officers Advanced Course at Fort Benning. He went to Fort Benning to

By 1975 the Powells had three children. From left to right, Annemarie (5), Linda (10), and Michael (12) are pictured here in this Powell family photo.

look for housing for his family. He found many houses in the nearby city of Columbus, but they would not rent to an African American. He had to look for a home in an African-American neighborhood.

Finally, Powell found a house in a neglected neighborhood. Unpainted shacks surrounded the nice brick house he found. It was ten miles from Fort Benning, but Powell was desperate to find a place for Alma and Michael. He rented the house and began to fix it up.

Powell and other African Americans were forced to use separate entrances to restaurants in the 1960s. This restaurant in Maryland is marked with a sign telling African Americans that they must use a rear entrance to the building.

One night he stayed late in the neighborhood working on the house. On the drive back to Fort Benning, Powell was tired and hungry. Knowing he would not be served in a restaurant because he was African American, Powell pulled up to a hamburger stand. He expected a waitress to come out and take his order as she would for any other customer. When a waitress arrived, she asked Powell if he was from another country. If he were, she said she would serve him. Powell told her he was American. She told him she was sorry, but he had to come to the back door for his food. Powell told her to forget it and drove away.

Back to Vietnam

In 1968 Powell was **assigned** once more to Vietnam. The war had grown much larger, and by the time Powell arrived in July, more than 500,000 American soldiers were fighting in Vietnam. Powell's job was to supply soldiers with ammunition and their helicopters with fuel. He also was in charge of making sure the soldiers got their mail.

In November Powell and his supervisor, Major General Charles Gettys flew by helicopter to see a large number of weapons their men had captured from enemy soldiers. As the pilot tried to land on a small field in the jungle, one of the helicopter's propeller blades hit a tree. The helicopter dropped to the ground and crashed. Fearing the helicopter would catch fire, Powell raced from the crash.

In 1968 Powell rescued Major General Charles Gettys and others after their helicopter crashed. Powell received the Soldier's Medal for bravery. The Soldier's Medal is awarded to individuals who act heroically in situations not involving actual battle.

Almost immediately, he noticed that the rest of the passengers had not escaped. He went back into the helicopter, and he and some other soldiers got everyone out. For his quick thinking and bravery, Powell earned the Soldier's Medal. In July of 1969, Powell left Vietnam for the last time.

Powell was awarded a Soldier's Medal (pictured) for his heroism in Vietnam. He also was given a Purple Heart and a Bronze Star during his military career.

Chapter 4:
Growing Success

In the fall of 1969, Powell enrolled in graduate school at George Washington University in Washington, D.C. He decided to study business administration, thinking he could find a job in the business world after he retired from the Army. He found his business courses very difficult. At 32, he was the oldest person in his classes, but he studied hard.

In May 1970 the Powells had their second daughter, Annemarie. Their first daughter, Linda, had been born in April 1965. Powell was so proud of Annemarie that he carried her down the street to show her off to his neighbors. Two months later, Powell received another **promotion** in the Army. He was now Lieutenant Colonel Powell.

A new command in South Korea

In 1950 North Korea **invaded** South Korea in an attempt to take over. The United States and fifteen other countries sent soldiers to help defend South Korea. This conflict became known as the Korean War (1950–1953).

After the war, a demilitarized zone was created between the countries. This strip of land was set up to protect South Korea from invasion and is off-limits to both North and South Korean armies. American soldiers still protect this zone today.

In 1973, two years after Powell graduated from George Washington University with a master's degree in business administration, Powell was **assigned** to go to South Korea. There he took charge of about 400 soldiers who were defending the demilitarized zone.

Powell saw that there were many problems at his **base** in Korea. About 18,000 soldiers were living at the base. Many were unhappy and bored. Some were using drugs. Powell worked with the general in charge to create programs to bring pride back to the soldiers. First, he kicked soldiers who were using drugs out of the Army. Then, he worked to get the rest of the soldiers into good physical shape. By the time Powell left Korea in September 1974, the men looked and acted like good soldiers. For the first time, Powell knew he could lead and inspire large groups of soldiers.

This sign marks the Military Demarcation Line within the United Nations controlled Demilitarized Zone separating North and South Korea.

Moving up

For the next several years, Powell continued his climb up the military ranks. In 1978 he was **promoted** to brigadier general. Five years later he was promoted to major general. Powell's knowledge of American wars and the United States Army made him very qualified for these promotions. More importantly, the soldiers in his **command** considered him a fair and experienced leader. Soon, his expertise would lead him to a new kind of work in the United States government.

Assistant to the secretary of defense

In 1983 Powell was called to Washington, D.C., to become the military assistant to Caspar Weinberger, the secretary of defense. Weinberger served as a military **adviser** to President Ronald Reagan. As the secretary's assistant, Powell planned and led meetings, gathered information, and scheduled the secretary's time.

From Weinberger, Powell learned much about how the government worked. For example, when Weinberger determined that the United States military needed more money, Powell helped prepare information to convince Congress to increase military funding. Using Powell's reports, Weinberger convinced members of Congress, and they voted to increase the amount of money they gave to the military. The money helped improve soldiers' pay and made the **bases** and equipment more modern.

National security advisor

In 1986, after some brief work in West Germany, Powell was **appointed** as deputy assistant to the president for national security affairs under President Reagan. In his new job, he would assist Frank Carlucci, an old friend and the new national security advisor.

For the first time, Powell had an office in the White House. He assisted Carlucci with problems that threatened the safety of the United States. They gathered information and gave advice to the president.

United States Secretary of Defense Caspar Weinberger speaks at a hearing held by the United States Senate on April 20, 1983. On the right, United States Secretary of State George Shultz listens.

President Reagan promoted Powell to national security advisor in 1987. Here, he is meeting with Reagan and Secretary of Defense Frank Carlucci on October 29, 1987.

In the fall of 1987, Frank Carlucci was **appointed** secretary of defense. President Reagan **promoted** Powell to national security **advisor**. Powell was the first African American in this position, and he knew that many African Americans would look up to him.

Powell served as national security advisor for a little more than one year. During that year, the leader of the Soviet Union, Mikhail Gorbachev, and President Reagan met to talk about reducing the number of **nuclear weapons** that the Soviet Union and the United States had. This meeting was very important because it was the first time in more than 40 years that the Soviet Union and the United States tried to **resolve** their differences.

Powell knew that if the Soviet Union and the United States could agree to reduce the amount of nuclear weapons each country had, both countries would be safer. He worked with the president to plan the meetings with Gorbachev. He wrote reports describing the weapons in detail. He talked to Soviet generals about how to reduce the number of weapons. In December 1987 President Reagan and Gorbachev signed the Intermediate-Range Nuclear Forces (INF) **Treaty**, an important agreement to reduce the number of nuclear weapons each country had. The treaty eliminated nuclear and ground-launched missiles with ranges of 300–3,400 miles (500–5,500 kilometers). Powell welcomed the INF Treaty as the first step toward a more peaceful world. By the treaty's deadline of June 1, 1991, a total of 2,692 weapons had been destroyed, 846 by the United States and 1,846 by the Soviet Union.

Ronald Reagan often met with Mikhail Gorbachev, the premier of the Soviet Union. The two leaders signed a treaty to reduce the number of nuclear weapons in the United States and the Soviet Union.

Chapter 5:
Top of the U.S. Military

When President Reagan left the White House in January 1989, Powell left his job as national security **adviser**. Once again, he returned to the United States Army. He was **promoted** to full general, and now he had four stars. Only two generals in history have had ever had five stars. The Army **assigned** Powell to Forces **Command** at Fort McPherson, Georgia. He was in charge of about one million soldiers based in the United States.

Chairman of the joint chiefs of staff

In August 1989 Secretary of Defense Dick Cheney recommended Powell be **appointed** the new chairman of the joint chiefs of staff. The joint chiefs of staff is a committee that includes a top official from each military branch, plus a chairman and deputy chairman. Through the chairman, the members of the committee advise the president, the secretary of defense, and the national security

In the fall of 1990 Powell was chairman of the joint chiefs of staff and Dick Cheney was the secretary of defense. Later, Cheney would become vice president.

council about military concerns. Chairman of the joint chiefs is the highest position available for a military officer.

Powell was the first African American to hold this position. At age 52, he was also the youngest. Powell was honored and eager to get to work studying military problems, listening to advice from the different branch chiefs, and offering advice.

General Benjamin O. Davis Jr. (1912–2002)

Benjamin O. Davis Jr. was the son of the first African-American general in the U.S. Army. He was born in 1912 in Washington, D.C. In 1932 he became the fourth African American to attend West Point Military Academy. He faced **discrimination** at West Point. Other **cadets** refused to speak to him or associate with him.

When he graduated from West Point in 1936, he applied to be a pilot. At the time, African Americans were not allowed to be pilots, so he was **assigned** to an all African-American troop at Fort Benning, Georgia.

During World War II, the U.S. Air Force created a flying course for African Americans at Tuskegee Institute in Tuskegee, Alabama. Davis was the commander of the first graduating class. He completed 60 **missions** in the war, and was awarded the Distinguished Flying Cross.

By the time Davis retired in 1970, he had earned three stars and was a major general in the Air Force. In 1998, President Clinton **promoted** him to full general and presented him with a fourth star. Davis is one of the many soldiers that Colin Powell admires.

Powell and other members of the cabinet of the President George H. W. Bush met on August 4, 1990, to discuss the invasion of Kuwait by Iraqi forces.

Operation Desert Storm

In August 1990, Saddam Hussein of Iraq **invaded** Kuwait, the country to the south of Iraq. Kuwait is a small country on the Persian Gulf. It is mostly a desert, but has a large natural oil supply. President Hussein claimed that part of Kuwait's oil fields belonged to Iraq. His soldiers quickly took over Kuwait.

Powell and the joint chiefs began to make plans to send United States troops to protect Kuwait. If Hussein refused to pull his troops out of Kuwait, Powell believed the United States needed to force them out. He hoped the **United Nations** might convince Hussein to leave. Soon though, everyone realized that Hussein planned to keep Iraqi soldiers in Kuwait.

Powell, the joint chiefs, and General H. Norman Schwarzkopf began to plan Operation Desert Storm. This conflict is also known as the Gulf War (1991). President George H. W. Bush brought many countries together to fight Iraq. Britain, France, Canada, Italy, and many Arab countries sent soldiers to help with the fighting.

The war begins

On January 16, 1991, the air war began. The United States sent more than 850 airplanes to bomb Iraq. The planes destroyed radio towers, weapons, and army **bases**. The night the war began, Powell stayed in his office all night. He could not sleep knowing he was sending young soldiers to war. He wanted to receive reports from General Schwarzkopf as soon as they came in.

For a little more than a month, U.S. warplanes pounded Iraq. Still, Iraqi troops did not leave Kuwait. On February 24, President Bush ordered the troops on the ground to attack. More than 500,000 U.S. soldiers and 200,000 **ally** soldiers were ready in the desert along Kuwait's border. They quickly captured more than 70,000 Iraqi soldiers, and Hussein ordered his troops to withdraw.

In less than four days after the ground attack began, Iraq pulled its soldiers out of Kuwait. The war was over quickly, but the fact that 147 American soldiers died in battle and another 236 soldiers were injured was of great concern to Colin Powell.

Retirement

In 1993 Powell finished his fourth year as chairman of the joint chiefs of staff. After more than 35 years in the military and in government, Powell wanted to retire. In September 1993, he dressed in his uniform for the last time. He arrived at Fort Meyer with Alma, his children, his sister, and her family. Many friends packed the parade grounds. U.S. President Bill Clinton presented Powell with the Presidential Medal of Freedom, an honor given to those who have contributed to the safety of the United States or world peace. President Clinton also gave Alma the Army's Decoration for Distinguished Civilian Service for her work with the Red Cross.

At the ceremony, the Army band played the "General Colin L. Powell March." Nineteen cannons fired a salute. Powell thought about his long career. He had risen from an army lieutenant to the chairman of the joint chiefs of staff. He had met presidents and leaders from around the world. He thanked everyone that day. Then he went home, took off his uniform, and looked forward to his new job of simply being Alma's husband.

Powell and General H. Norman Schwarzkopf planned Operation Desert Storm. They are shown here on February 10, 1991.

Powell and his wife, Alma, are pictured here at Powell's retirement ceremony in 1993. Powell spent more than 35 years in the United States Army.

Chapter 6: Secretary of State

Whenever Powell wanted to relax, he worked on old cars. Taking out old engines, changing oil, and getting cars running made him happy. Not long after he retired, Powell was driving on the freeway in Washington, D.C., when he ran out of gas. A man helped him push his old car onto the shoulder.

Powell realized that he no longer had a large staff of 90 assistants to help him. A police officer drove up and gave him enough gas to get off the freeway. When he got off the freeway, he got caught in a traffic jam and ran out of gas again. He found humor in the situation—he had once been the most powerful man in the United States military, but he could not remember to put gas in his car.

Powell enjoyed his retirement. In December 1993 he was invited to meet Queen Elizabeth of England. Queen Elizabeth

Powell is shown on September 23, 1996, signing his autobiography for an admirer.

awarded him the Knight Commander of the Order of the Bath. Because he was American, he did not kneel down to be knighted, as is the custom for people receiving this honor. Instead, the Queen handed him his award and invited him and Alma to sit down and talk.

In 1995 Powell wrote a book about his life called *My American Journey*. He traveled around the United States giving speeches to students and business professionals. He especially enjoyed talking to groups of young students. He spent time with his family, listened to music, and read books. Powell did everything he never had time to do when he was working.

Secretary of state

In the fall of 2000, George W. Bush was elected president of the United States. Bush knew Colin Powell had worked for his father, President George H. W. Bush. In December George W. Bush asked Powell to serve as his secretary of state. After the U.S. Senate approved his **appointment**, Powell became secretary of state on January 20, 2001.

The secretary of state is one of the most important positions in the White House. The secretary advises the president on **foreign policy**. Foreign policy is the strategy the United States has for maintaining relationships with other countries.

Terrorists attack the United States

On the morning of September 11, 2001, **terrorists** attacked the United States. They attacked the World Trade Center in New York City and the Pentagon building near Washington, D.C. More than 3,000 Americans died in these attacks. This was the first time since World War II that anyone had attacked the United States at home.

Powell was meeting with the president of Peru when he heard about the attack. He returned to the United States right away. He planned to talk to leaders around the world to find out who was responsible for the attacks.

Powell is seen in the background of this photo as President George W. Bush speaks to reporters about the terrorist attacks on September 11, 2001.

The following week, Powell met with President Bush, the secretary of defense, and many military **advisers**. Powell advised the president on how to react to the **terrorists**. Most advisers believed that the attacks were planned by Osama bin Laden, the leader of the terrorist group Al Qaeda, who was thought to be living in country called Afghanistan. President Bush asked Powell and his advisers to plan a way to capture bin Laden.

War in Afghanistan

Afghanistan is in south Asia, between Pakistan and Iran. From 1998 until 2001, a group called the Taliban had control of Afghanistan. The Taliban was protecting bin Laden. President Bush asked them to turn bin Laden over to the United States. The leaders of the Taliban refused. On October 7, 2001, the United States attacked Afghanistan.

Many countries joined the Americans in the fight. President Bush and Powell convinced Great Britain, Australia, Russia, and Pakistan to support the war. Soon, the Afghan people joined the war to force the Taliban to leave. They successfully overthrew the Taliban, but bin Laden was not found. In December, Powell worked with Afghan leaders to set up a new government. He also made sure that food and emergency supplies were shipped in.

Fighting terrorism

After the terrorist attacks on September 11th, President Bush declared a "war on terror." He intended to rid the world of anyone who might attack the United States and its **allies** as Osama bin Laden had.

Terrorism is very difficult to fight. Small groups of terrorists plan attacks on many different countries. Sometimes they die in the attacks. They are more difficult to fight than enemies who wear uniforms and fight for their countries. Powell believes the war against terrorists may take many years to win.

Powell answers questions from United States senators on May 8, 2001, regarding the U.S. government's ability to combat terrorism.

War with Iraq

In 2002 President Bush decided that Saddam Hussein, the president of Iraq, was a danger to the United States. Powell went to the **United Nations** to ask the countries of the world to force Iraq to get rid of its dangerous weapons. Powell understood the danger. He had planned the Gulf War against Hussein in 1991. The United Nations gave Hussein a deadline to turn over its dangerous weapons.

Powell hoped that Hussein would agree to work with the United Nations. He did not want to go to war again. When Hussein did not turn over any weapons, the United States began to bomb Iraq on March 19, 2003. They then **invaded** Iraq and captured Baghdad, the capital city. On May 1, 2003, President Bush announced that the major battles were over, though Saddam Hussein had not yet been caught. Eventually, on December 13, Hussein was captured by American troops. However, in 2005, the war with Iraq was still being fought, as the United States tried to help a new government take over in Iraq.

In 2004 President Bush was elected to a second term as president. Colin Powell decided that after four years as secretary of state, it was time for him to resign. He is now, once again, a private citizen. Powell was replaced as secretary of state by Condoleezza Rice. Rice is the first African-American woman and only the second woman to become secretary of state.

Powell is shown here on March 26, 2003, in Washington, D.C. On November 15, 2004, he would resign as secretary of state.

Chapter 7:
Colin Powell's Place in History

Colin Powell has led a remarkable life. He has achieved the highest level in the United States military. He has also served in the highest government positions of any African American in history. He is aware of his good fortune and thanks the U.S. Army for offering equal opportunities for all Americans. When Powell retired from the military in 1993, he said, "My only regret was that I could not do it all over again."

Many people have asked Powell to run for president of the United States. He thought about it in 1995. He discussed it with his wife and family. He was retired at the time, and Alma liked having him home. He liked the freedom to choose his work. In the end, he decided not to run for president, but he could still run in the future.

In 1997 Powell helped form a group called America's Promise. This organization looks for ways to improve the lives of young people in the United States. America's Promise was the idea of many people. All the living former presidents of the United States met in Philadelphia to launch America's Promise. Presidents Bill Clinton, George H. W. Bush, Jimmy Carter, and Gerald Ford came together. Nancy Reagan represented her husband, Ronald Reagan, who was too sick to attend the conference. Hundreds of other community leaders were also there from all over the nation.

At this meeting the presidents asked the country to make children and youth a priority. They then joined Powell in officially starting the new organization. It was to be called America's Promise—The Alliance for Youth.

Powell knows that life is difficult for many American children. General Powell's own life had taught him how important it was to believe in himself in order to reach his goals. He wanted America's Promise to help young people all over the United States believe in themselves so they could have the best lives possible. This is one way that he passed on the values that his own parents gave him. America's Promise tries to make sure that every child has a safe, healthy, and happy place to grow up. As part of this goal, Powell asks young people to volunteer and help others.

On November 12, 2004, Colin Powell announced that he would resign as secretary of state. At the age of 67, he was ready to return to a private life. President George W. Bush called him "one of the great public servants of our time." He praised Colin Powell as a soldier, a diplomat, a statesman, and a patriot.

Powell served his country for more than 40 years. He has faced many challenges during his career, but he never gave up when life became difficult. He sees problems as challenges that he must work hard to overcome. Colin Powell's loyalty to his country and his respect for public service have always inspired him to do his best.

Glossary

adviser/advisor person who gives someone information and advice

ally country that gives support to another, especially during a war

appoint to fill a position in a government or other organization without an election

assignment job for military officers

base place where soldiers are trained and live while in the military

cadet person training in the military

command people, area, or unit under a commander

communism system of government in which all property is owned by the government and all people have an equal share of the land and businesses. A communist is a person who believes in communism.

discrimination treatment of some people better than others without a proper or fair reason

drill team group of people who march and perform together to display their military skills

ethnic group group of people who share a common race, language, and culture

foreign policy way one country's government acts toward another

geology science that deals with the history of Earth and its life, especially as recorded in rocks

immigrant person who moves to a new country to live there

infantry soldiers trained to fight on foot; a part of an army

invade forcefully enter another country

mission military task

nuclear weapon weapon with enormous destructive power that gets its energy from nuclear reactions

promote to move up in rank or position

resolve find an answer or solution to

terrorism violent attack made to achieve a goal and frighten people. A terrorist is a person who uses terrorism.

treaty agreement between two or more countries

United Nations organization that brings countries together to solve disagreements

Timeline

1937 Colin Powell is born in Harlem on April 5.

1954 Graduates from Morris High School in February 1954.
Enrolls at the City College of New York.
Joins the Reserve Officers Training Corps.

1958 Graduates from the City College of New York.

1962 Powell marries Alma Johnson in August.

1963 Colin and Alma have a son, Michael, in March.

1965 Colin and Alma have a daughter, Linda, in April.

1968 Returns to Vietnam for a year.
Rescues Major General Gettys in a helicopter crash.

1970 The Powells have their second daughter, Annemarie, in May.
Promoted to lieutenant colonel.

1978 Promoted to brigadier general and receives his first star.

1983 Becomes top military assistant to Caspar Weinberger, the
secretary of defense. Promoted to major general and receives
his second star.

1987 Appointed national security **adviser.**

1989 Appointed chairman of the Joint Chiefs of Staff.
Promoted to full general.

1993 Powell retires from the Army.

2001 Powell is sworn in as the 65th U.S. secretary of state on January 20.

2004 Powell resigns as secretary of state.

Further Information

Further reading

Dunn, John M. *The Vietnam War: A History of U.S. Involvement.* San Diego: Lucent Books, 2001.

Finlayson, Reggie. *Colin Powell: People's Hero.* Minneapolis: Lerner Publications, 1997.

Flanagan, Alice K. *Colin Powell: U.S. Army General and Secretary of State.* Chicago: Ferguson Publishing, 2001.

Haskins, James. *African American Military Heroes.* New York: John Wiley & Sons, 1998.

Wukovits, John F. *Colin Powell.* San Diego: Lucent Books, 2000.

Addresses

America's Promise—The Alliance for Youth
909 N. Washington Street, Suite 400
Alexandria, VA 22314-1556

Buffalo Soldiers National Museum
1834 Southmore
Houston, TX 77004

U.S. Army Center of Military History
 ATTD: DAMH-MD
103 Third Avenue, N.W.
Fort McNair
Washington, D.C. 20319-5058

Index

5/06 8E